GrV

Expe

MATERIAL AND MATTER

with Toys and Everyday Stuff
BY NATALIE ROMPELLA

Raintree is an imprint of Capstone Global Library Limited, a company incorporated in England and Wales having its registered office at 7 Pilgrim Street, London, EC4V 6LB – Registered company number: 6695582

www.raintree.co.uk
myorders@raintree.co.uk

Edited by Alesha Sullivan
Designed by Kyle Grenz
Picture research by Jo Miller
Production by Kathy McColley

ISBN 978 1 474 70356 7 (hardback)
19 18 17 16 15
10 9 8 7 6 5 4 3 2 1

ISBN 978 1 474 70361 1 (paperback)
20 19 18 17 16
10 9 8 7 6 5 4 3 2 1

British Library Cataloguing in Publication Data
A full catalogue record for this book is available from the British Library.

Acknowledgements
Capstone Studio/Karon Dubke except: Shutterstock: Budkov, 4 (volcano), cristi180884, cover (crayons), Nick Kinney, 11 (hot air balloons), PlusONE, 4 (pebbles), Svetlana Lukienko, 4 (steaming cup)

We would like to thank Paul Ohmann, PhD, Associate Professor of Physics at the University of St. Thomas in St. Paul, Minnesota, for his invaluable help in the preparation of this book.

Printed and bound in China.

CONTENTS

Turn your house
into a science lab!........... 4

Vehicle weighing station 6

That's a sinker!.......... 8

Gas-powered car............. 10

Dry those clothes!............12

Egg-splosion 14

Melting matter................. 16

What's the matter
with this matter?............ 18

Why it works............. 20

Glossary   22
Read more   23
Websites........... 23
Index 24

TURN YOUR HOUSE INTO A SCIENCE LAB!

Our world is made up of **matter**. It makes up everything from a football to a lollipop to a crayon. Matter comes in three forms: **liquid**, **solid** and **gas**.

Examples of liquids:
water, shampoo, lava from a volcano

Examples of solids:
books, rocks, ice

Examples of gases:
steam from a hot cup of tea, air inside a blown-up balloon

matter anything that has weight and takes up space
liquid matter that is wet and can be poured, such as water
solid matter that holds its shape
gas matter that is not solid or liquid; a gas can move about freely and does not have a definite shape

We drink matter, breathe matter and best of all, we play with matter. You can learn all about matter through fun experiments. All you need are some toys and objects from around your house!

Safety first!

You may need an adult's help for some of these experiments. But most of them can be done on your own. If you have a question about how to do a step safely, make sure you ask an adult. Think safety first!

TURN TO PAGE 20 TO SEE HOW THE SCIENCE WORKS IN EACH EXPERIMENT!

VEHICLE WEIGHING STATION

Matter has weight. Sometimes it's important to know the weight of objects. For example, fruit and vegetables are weighed at the supermarket. Create your own **balance scale** to weigh your toy cars and lorries!

Materials:

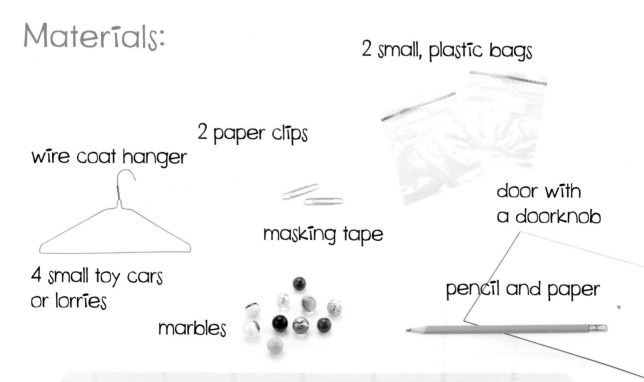

2 small, plastic bags

2 paper clips

wire coat hanger

door with a doorknob

masking tape

4 small toy cars or lorries

pencil and paper

marbles

balance scale instrument used for weighing things; when two objects are balanced, they weigh the same

Steps:

1. Create a balance scale by bending the paper clips open into the shape of an "S". Hook them around the bottom corners of a coat hanger. Tape them in place.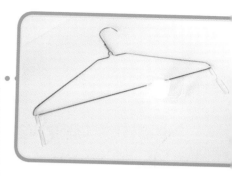

2. Connect a bag to the open end of one of the paper clips by poking the top through the paper clip. Make sure the bag can still open. Do the same on the other side of the hanger.

3. Hang your scale on a doorknob.

4. Place one toy car inside the bag on one side of the scale. Add marbles slowly to the other side until the scale is even. Write down how many marbles you needed to balance the two sides.

5. Repeat these steps for the other cars or toys. Which of your toys is the heaviest? Were there any that balanced using the same number of marbles?

THAT'S A SINKER!

Matter can do all sorts of fun things. Some types of matter stick to a magnet. Some can bend, such as rubber. Some matter **floats** in a liquid. But it can be hard to guess what will happen to an object in water. Do you have toys that you think will sink or float in water?

Materials:

Ask an adult to help you choose 8 to 10 toys that are water-resistant

sink or large container of water

Tip:
Don't use any battery-operated or electronic toys.

float stay on the surface of a liquid or in the air

Steps:

1. **Sort the toys into two piles, those you think will sink and those you think will float.**

2. **Fill your sink or a large container with water.**

3. **One by one, place each toy in the water. Which toy sinks and which toy floats? Were your guesses right? What do you think made some toys float and some toys sink?**

9

GAS-POWERED CAR

You might think you can see all types of matter. But we often can't see gas. Gas does not have a shape, and it can move freely. Oxygen that we breathe is a gas. Do you think you could use gas in a balloon to power one of your toy cars? Give it a try!

Materials:

tape

small toy car

a drinking straw cut in half

rubber band

a deflated balloon

Tip:

The bigger you blow up the balloon, the further your car will travel. You may need an adult's help blowing up the balloon.

Steps:

1. Place the end of the straw inside the opening of the balloon. Secure the balloon's opening tightly with the rubber band.

2. Tape the middle of the straw to the top of the car, near the front. Leave enough space on the other end of the straw so you can blow into it.

3. Blow up the balloon and hold the end of the straw closed with your finger.

4. Put the car on the ground and let go of the end of the straw. What happened to the car?

Fact:

Gas can also move really large objects, such as hot air balloons. The first hot air balloon took flight in 1783 in Paris, France.

DRY THOSE CLOTHES!

Have you ever noticed how a drinking glass gets beads of water on the outside of it when a room is warm? This process is called **condensation**. Or on a hot day, has your wet swimming costume ever dried on its own? The water in your swimming costume disappeared because of **evaporation**. In this easy experiment, you can see both in action!

Materials:

water

a sock, doll's clothes or a flannel

empty plastic container with a clear lid

condensation change from a gas to a liquid
evaporation change from a liquid to a gas

Steps:

1. **Soak the piece of clothing. Place it in the plastic container and shut the lid.**

2. **Put the container in the sunshine for 2 to 3 hours.**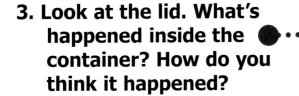

3. **Look at the lid. What's happened inside the container? How do you think it happened?**

Tip:

If you can't go outside, put the container by a window or in a warm room.

13

EGG-SPLOSION

Water is a powerful force, especially when it *freezes*. Water that gets into cracks in a road and then freezes can cause the road to split apart. See how powerful water can be when it changes from a liquid to a solid using a few simple supplies!

Materials:

plastic egg

small, plastic re-sealable bag

bowl of water

Tip:
Never put something in the freezer that could explode or shatter, such as a glass container.

freeze become solid or icy at a very low temperature

Steps:

1. If there are holes in the ends of the plastic egg, cover them with tape. Open the plastic egg. Submerge the egg in the bowl of water until it is full of water, and then shut the egg.

2. Place the egg in a plastic bag in case it leaks.

3. Freeze for 4 to 5 hours.

4. Check the egg. What happened to the water inside the egg?

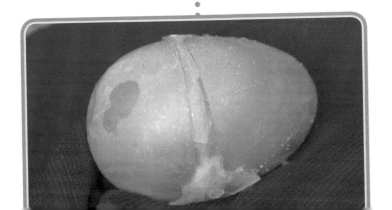

MELTING MATTER

Your toys are all made from different kinds of matter. Some toy cars are made of metal. Interlocking toy bricks are made of plastic. Crayons are made of wax. Metal, plastic and wax can all be **melted** down and poured into a **mould** to make objects we use every day. Try making new crayons by melting down your old ones!

Materials:

oven

foil baking cases

old cupcake tin

oven gloves

old or broken crayons

paper

Did you know that almost 87,000 LEGO® pieces are moulded every minute? Plastic is warmed up to a temperature between 232 and 310 degrees Celsius (450 and 590 degrees Fahrenheit) so that it melts. The plastic is then poured into a mould. It only takes 5 to 10 seconds for a LEGO® piece to cool down.

Steps:

1. Ask an adult to pre-heat the oven to 110° C (225° F).

2. Place the cupcake cases in the tin.

3. Remove the wrappers from old or broken crayons. Break the crayons into smaller pieces.

4. Place the crayons into the cupcake cases until they are half full.

5. Ask an adult to put the tin in the oven. Leave it in the oven for 10 minutes or until the crayons have completely melted. Ask an adult to remove the tin from the oven. Leave it to cool.

6. Remove the moulded crayons from the foil cases. Colour away!

melt change from a solid to a liquid
mould container for making liquid things
form a special shape when they harden

WHAT'S THE MATTER WITH THIS MATTER?

If liquids flow and solids hold a shape, is jam a solid or a liquid? What about whipped cream? Not all matter is easy to call a solid, liquid or gas. Can you work out which type of matter this mystery **mixture** is?

Materials:

piece of cardboard

spoon

toy car

60 grams cornflour

30 millilitres water (green food colouring optional)

toy hammer

small ball

shallow cake tin

mixture something made of different things mixed together

Steps:

1. Lay out a piece of cardboard on your work space.

2. Using a spoon, mix together the cornflour and water in a shallow cake tin and stir. Make sure you stir all the way to the bottom. Is the mixture a solid or a liquid? ●·············

3. Place a toy car on the mixture. Does the car sink or stay above the surface? Now drive the car through it. Does it sink or stay above the surface? ●·············

4. Hit the mixture with a toy hammer. Does it splash like a liquid?

5. Try bouncing a ball on the surface. Does it bounce? Would you say ●···· this mixture is a solid or a liquid?

Tip:

When you have finished with your mixture, throw it away carefully. Do not tip it down the sink. The water and cornflour will eventually separate, and the cornflour could block the drain.

WHY IT WORKS

Would you like to know how these amazing experiments work? Here is the science behind the fun!

PAGE 6 - VEHICLE WEIGHING STATION

The balance scale compared objects with another weight, in this case, the marbles. If the side with the object was lower than the side with the marbles, it weighed more than the marbles. If the side with the object was higher than the side with the marbles, it weighed less. When the two sides of the scale were equal, the object weighed the same as the marbles.

PAGE 8 - THAT'S A SINKER!

An object will float or sink depending on its weight and size. This is called its **density**. If the object was denser than water, it sank. If it was less dense than water, it floated.

PAGE 10 - GAS-POWERED CAR

Because the balloon isn't tied up, the air inside (which is a gas) pushed out of the balloon. The rushing air caused the toy car to move forward.

PAGE 12 - DRY THOSE CLOTHES!

As the water in the container heated up in the sunshine, it turned into **water vapour**. The vapour was trapped on the container lid. As it touched the lid and cooled, the vapour turned into water again.

PAGE 14 - EGG-SPLOSION

When the water turned from a liquid into a solid, the ice had nowhere to go. The water **expanded** when it froze. This pressure forced the egg open.

PAGE 16 - MELTING MATTER

The heat inside the oven melted the crayons from a solid to a liquid. As a liquid, they took the shape of the container they were in. As the crayons cooled, they became solid again and formed one large crayon.

PAGE 18 - WHAT'S THE MATTER WITH THIS MATTER?

Adding water to cornflour creates a mixture. Tiny pieces in the grains of cornflour lock up and become hard. The molecules make the mixture more like a solid than a liquid.

density how heavy or light an object is in relation to its size
water vapour water in gas form
expand get bigger

GLOSSARY

balance scale instrument used for weighing things; when two objects are balanced, they weigh the same

condensation change from a gas to a liquid

density how heavy or light an object is in relation to its size

evaporation change from a liquid to a gas

expand get bigger

float stay on the surface of a liquid or in the air

freeze become solid or icy at a very low temperature

gas matter that is not solid or liquid; a gas can move about freely and does not have a definite shape

liquid matter that is wet and can be poured, such as water

matter anything that has weight and takes up space

melt change from a solid to a liquid

mixture something made of different things mixed together

mould container for making liquid things form a special shape when they harden

solid matter that holds its shape

water vapour water in gas form

READ MORE

All About Earth (Discover Earth Science), Sara Latta (Raintree, 2015)

Experiments with Heating and Cooling (Read and Experiment), Isabel Thomas (Raintree, 2015)

Plastic (Exploring Materials), Abby Colich (Raintree, 2013)

WEBSITES

www.bbc.co.uk/bitesize/ks2/science/materials/
Discover more experiments that explore and reveal the properties of solids, liquids and gases.

http://ngkids.co.uk/science-and-nature/water-cycle
For more information about condensation and evaporation and some amazing water facts, visit the National Geographic children's website.

INDEX

balance scales 6-7, 20
balloons 4, 10-11, 20

condensation 12
crayons 4, 16-17, 21

density 20

evaporation 12

floating 8-9, 20
freezing 14-15

gases 4, 10-11, 18, 20

heating 17, 21

liquids 4, 8, 14, 18-19, 21

magnets 8
marbles 6-7, 20
melting 16-17, 21
metals 16
mixtures 18-19, 21

molecules 21
moulds 16-17

oxygen 10

roads 14

sinking 8-9, 19, 20
solids 4, 14, 18-19, 21

water vapour 21
wax 16